The Rockwool Foundation Research Unit

Useful beautiful minds
– An analysis of the relationship between schizophrenia and employment

Jane Greve and Louise Herrup Nielsen

University Press of Southern Denmark
Odense 2012

Useful beautiful minds – An analysis of the relationship between schizophrenia and employment

Study Paper No. 44

Published by:
© The Rockwool Foundation Research Unit and
University Press of Southern Denmark

Copying from this book is permitted only within institutions that have agreements with CopyDan, and only in accordance with the limitations laid down in the agreement

Address:
The Rockwool Foundation Research Unit
Sølvgade 10, 2.tv
DK-1307 Copenhagen K

Telephone   +45 33 34 48 00

Fax   +45 33 34 48 99

E-mail   forskningsenheden@rff.dk

Home page   www.rff.dk

ISBN 978-87-90199-76-0
ISSN 0908-3979
November 2012
Print run: 350
Printed by   Specialtrykkeriet Viborg

Price: 60.00 DKK, including 25 % VAT

Contents

1 Introduction.. 6
2 Background.. 8
3 Data.. 10
4 Methodological approach 14
5 Results.. 16
    5.1 The employment rate 15 years before and 10 years after admission or selection 16
    5.2 Schizophrenia and employment 18
    5.3 Age at First Admission 22
    5.4 Length of First Admission 24
6. Discussion 26
7. Conclusion.. 26
References 28
Appendix 30

Useful beautiful minds – An analysis of the relationship between schizophrenia and employment

Jane Greve[a]* and Louise Herrup Nielsen[a]

Abstract: This paper examines the relationship between schizophrenia and employment. While most other studies have used cross-sectional data to estimate this relationship, we use longitudinal register data and show the development in the employment rate of people with schizophrenia 15 years before the first admission to a psychiatric hospital until 10 years after this admission. We find a considerable drop in the employment rate for people with schizophrenia six years before the first hospitalization and the employment rate stabilizes at 18 % after the first admission.

As family and neighborhood environment can be important factors in the development of mental illnesses and labor market outcomes, we use sibling fixed effects to estimate the relationship between schizophrenia and employment. The difference in the employment rate in 2007 for the siblings with and without schizophrenia is estimated at 67 %. This difference is reduced to 56 % when we include control variables such as marital status, educational achievement and work experience but remain unchanged when we apply a sibling fixed effect approach which controls for unobserved family specific characteristics that the siblings share.

Keywords: Severe mental disorder, Employment, Danish administrative data, Sibling fixed effects
JEL codes: I10, J21

[a] Rockwool Foundation Research Unit, Sølvgade 10, 2. tv., 1307 Copenhagen K, Denmark
* Corresponding author: tel: +45 3334 4806 fax:+45 3334 4899; email adress: jg@rff.dk

1 Introduction

"To some extent, sanity is a form of conformity. And to some extent, people who are insane are non-conformists and society and their family wishes [....] that they would live what appear to be useful lives. They would work. They would earn money." (Interview with John Nash, Nobel Prize winner in Economic Sciences in 1994. John Nash was diagnosed with paranoid schizophrenia in 1959.)

Schizophrenia is a severe mental disorder that disturbs the mind and behavior for the individual affected. Not surprisingly, all previous literature (Marwaha & Johnson, 2004) find a low employment rate among people with schizophrenia. As most people with schizophrenia receive the diagnosis at a very young age (Sham, MacLean & Kendler, 1994), they often have a lifelong dependence on public transfers. However, developments in psychiatric treatment over the last 15-20 years have made recovery more likely. Recent research shows that 50% of newly diagnosed schizophrenics will be free of symptoms after 2 years – and 20% will be able to participate in work or education at the same level as before they began showing symptoms related to schizophrenia (Nordentoft, 2009). Although a significant amount of people with schizophrenia are unable to hold a job, a significant number of people with schizophrenia either work or could work, depending on their symptoms. Furthermore, a significant fraction of people with schizophrenia consider employment and education the most important factors in their recovery process and, when they consider employment, they prefer an ordinary job to sheltered employment (Christensen & Nordentoft, 2011).

Although a well-established negative relationship between schizophrenia and employment exists (see Mawaha & Johnson, 2004, for a review of the literature), several limitations in the literature do not allow us to draw conclusions about the causal relationship between schizophrenia and employment. First, most previous literature uses cross-sectional data in estimating the relationship between schizophrenia and employment. However, mental illnesses may develop gradually while the labor market attachment simultaneously deteriorates. A study by Agerbo et al. (2004) uses longitudinal data and follows schizophrenic patients up to 10 years before their first hospitalization. They find that up to 10 years prior to the first hospital admission these patients were more frequently living alone, unemployed and receiving social assistance than a control group of the same average age and gender and that the percentage increases gradually over time.

Second, a possible third factor that affects both the development of schizophrenia and employment might lead to (omitted variable) bias in the relationship between schizophrenia and employment as found in the previous literature. Although it is possible to control for variables that might influence both schizophrenia and employment, such as education and work experience, many of these variable might be affected by symptoms of schizophrenia before the diagnosis and might therefore be less relevant when we estimate the effect of schizophrenia on employment. Instead, early childhood factors, such as the family and neighborhood environment, might be important for estimates of the impact of schizophrenia on employment. Both parental socioeconomic characteristics in early childhood and a disadvantaged home environment have been shown to be important for the probability of developing severe mental disorders, (McLaughlin, 2011) and a long list of studies has shown that early childhood factors are related to later employment (see, e.g., Heckman & Masterov, 2007).

This paper contributes to the literature on the relationship between schizophrenia and employment in several ways. First, while previous literature have usually used cross-sectional data when estimating the relationship between schizophrenia and employment, we add to this literature by using Danish administrative register data from 1980 to 2007 on psychiatric patients in Denmark. With this data set, we are able to show the development in the employment rate among people with schizophrenia up to 15 years before and 10 years after the first hospitalization. Second, we show the difference in the employment rate between siblings with and without schizophrenia. When we compare siblings with and without schizophrenia, we are able to eliminate omitted factors shared by the sibling pairs, such as family and neighborhood characteristics. Thus we examine whether confounders and shared unobserved family specific characteristics explain the previous results linking schizophrenia and employment.

Third, while additional information on demographic and socioeconomic status in most studies relies on information from surveys, we have merged the data set on psychiatric records with a long list of other administrative register data, including detailed information on family relations, educational attainment, work experience, criminal records and hospitalization. Fourth, as the correlation between schizophrenia and employment might differ across heterogeneous groups, we test the robustness of the average correlation between schizophrenia and employment by examining two flexible specifications of schizophrenia: age at first admission and length of stay at the hospital at first admission.

Our results show an increasing gap in the employment rates for siblings with and without schizophrenia from up to 15 years before the first hospital admission. Siblings with schizophrenia show a considerable drop in the employment rate six years before the first hospitalization. After the first hospital admission, the employment rate stabilizes at approximately 18% for the siblings with schizophrenia. The difference in the employment rate in 2007 between the siblings with and without schizophrenia is estimated to be 67 percentage points. This result remains unchanged in the sibling fixed effect approach, indicating that the coefficient to schizophrenia is not biased by unobserved family characteristics shared by the siblings. Moreover, when we examined heterogeneous effects across the age at and the length of the first admission, respectively, we found that the average difference in the employment rate was relatively robust to different admission ages and admission lengths. However, the difference in the employment rate is larger if the individuals are admitted between ages 25-30.

Although not conclusive, the results in this paper are policy relevant along at least one dimension. The decrease in the employment rate many years before the group is diagnosed with schizophrenia could indicate stigma or productivity loss from the illness through depreciating human and social capital. The more the human and social capital depreciates, the more the individual may become alienated from the labor market or simply lose his or her contacts within it. The marginalizing effects appear persistent, and early interventions that reduce these symptoms might have important effects on employment.

2 Background

Patients with schizophrenia are most often characterized by psychotic symptoms. These symptoms suggest that they often lose contact with reality, including having false ideas about what is taking place or who they are. As schizophrenia is thus a disabling disease when not treated many people with schizophrenia in Denmark are eligible for early retirement. In 2005, for example, 53 and 43 % among men and women aged 25-to 40-years old with schizophrenia, respectively, were not employed and almost all of them were receiving early retirement benefits (Greve, 2012).

The consequences of schizophrenia for individuals, their close family and friends, and society at large are huge. In Europe, the total mental health costs are estimated to be 3-4% of GDP. Of these costs, 75-80% is estimated to be indirect costs, including costs related to reduced productivity, increased absenteeism, work disability, long-term unemployment, early retirement, and reduced investment in and return on human capital. Costs related to schizophrenia are significant and large in Denmark. A comparative study of Denmark, the Netherlands, the UK, Italy, and Spain shows that Denmark has the largest costs associated with schizophrenia per patient (Andlin-Sobocki et al., 2005).

There is evidence that people with schizophrenia want to work (Bates, 1996; Hatfield et al., 1992), but also that few of them do so (Mawaha & Johnson, 2004). The lower probability of being employed for people with schizophrenia can be explained by employer-determined factors. Conditions related to the person with schizophrenia may imply that the employer cannot or will not hire a person with schizophrenia, either because there have to be special circumstances for a person with this mental disorder, adding costs for the employer or because the employer anticipates such costs. Jacobsen et al. (2010) refers to schizophrenia as one of the most stigmatizing mental illnesses. In this qualitative study about stigmas related to schizophrenia, persons with schizophrenia are described with words such as "incurable", "irresponsible", "violent outward reacting behavior" and "crime" (Jacobsen et al., 2010). If these characteristics are the general perception of people with schizophrenia, it is likely that people with schizophrenia may also experience direct discrimination if their employer knows about their condition.

Previous literature on the relationship between severe mental illness and labor market status appears to agree that severe psychiatric disorders reduce the probability of being employed. However, the results differ depending on the type of disorder, type of measurement and estimation methods (Bartel et al., 1979; Chatterji et al., 2011; Ettner et al., 1997; Marcotte et al., 2001; Marwaha & Johnson, 2004). At least two key challenges exist for estimating the relationship between severe mental illnesses and labor market status. The first challenge relates to measuring mental illnesses. This challenge includes identifying the symptoms and the specific diseases. Obtaining correct information (if any) from people in a severe stage of their mental illness is difficult. Consequently, conclusions are often based on selected samples when studies are based on surveys. Furthermore, assuming homogenous effects in the samples of pooled but fundamentally different diseases, may bias conclusions in arbitrary directions.

The second challenge is related to the problems estimating the causal effect of the specific psychiatric disorders on labor market outcomes, as psychiatric disorders might develop simultaneously with a deterioration of the position in the labor market, and unobserved factors might affect both the development of schizophrenia and employment. Previous studies have shown that mental illnesses tend to develop gradually and that labor market attachment simultaneously deteriorates. Agerbo et al. (2004) find that schizophrenic patients were more frequently unemployed up to 10 years prior to the first hospital admission than a control group with same gender and average age. Westergaard-Nielsen et al. (2004) examine the employment rate among a group of people hospitalized for a mental disorder and find that the employment rate drops significantly 5 years before the first hospitalization. Previous literature has handled the issues of reverse causality and omitted variable bias in cross-sectional data by applying an instrumental variable method (Chatterji et al., 2011; Ettner et al., 1997; Marcotte et al. 2001) or by using restrictions on the correlation coefficient and the functional form (Chatterji et al., 2011).[1]

---

[1] The results in Chartterji et al. (2011), which are based on a survey, show that past year psychiatric disorder is associated with reductions of 14 and 13 percent in the employment among men and women, respectively.

However, the results from the literature on pooled measures of mental disorder and employment status might not be valid for people with schizophrenia. This paper focuses on the relationship between schizophrenia and employment status. We use longitudinal data to observe the development in the employment rate before and after the first admission. When we estimate the employment rate, we include a list of variables to control for factors related to both schizophrenia and employment, factors omitted in descriptive studies such as Agerbo et al. (2004). By comparing siblings, we control for unobserved family and neighborhood characteristics shared between siblings. These factors could prove important, as schizophrenia usually develops at a young age. Finally, after finding evidence of a relationship between schizophrenia and employment, we explore more flexible definitions of schizophrenia – age and length of first hospitalization – to test the robustness of this relationship.

3 Data

We construct the data by merging the Danish Psychiatric Central Register (DPCR) with various Danish administrative registers from Statistic Denmark. The DPCR contains date of all admissions, discharges, and the primary psychiatric diagnosis.[2]

The Danish administrative register data is particularly useful for studying the relationship between schizophrenia and labor market status. As all Danish psychiatric hospitals are public, all admissions and discharges are recorded in the registers. Furthermore, treatments at the psychiatric hospitals in Denmark are free. Thus we have no attrition in our data set, and the people that most surveys do not cover, e.g., those with very severe cases of schizophrenia or those among the very lowest and highest socioeconemic groups, are included in the analysis. Moreover, the use of Danish register data allow us to compare siblingss and to control for a long list of covariates in the estimated models.

Since January 1995, information on all psychiatric outpatient contacts has been included in the DPCR leading to a dramatic increase in psychiatric patients. Thus

---

2 The Danish Psychiatric Central Register is described in details in Mors, Perto & Mortensen (2011). In 1994 the International Classification of Diseases (ICD) system changed from ICD-8 to ICD-10 in Denmark, implying that some mental disease can be diagnosed differently before and after January 1, 1994. Furthermore, there have been various other changes in the classification, when new diseases have been included and old diseases have been divided into other diseases. Thus, a comparison of diagnoses over time can be problematic. However, several studies find evidence that because of its severe nature, schizophrenia is one of the few mental disorders that are comparable over time (Munk-Jørgensen et al., 2000).

the data contain more patients with schizophrenia from 1995. The validity of the diagnoses in the register is examined in several studies (Laursen et al., 2012).

We selected a sample of all people aged 35-45, living in Denmark in 2007, who have been admitted to a psychiatric hospital and diagnosed with schizophrenia at least once from 1981 to 2007, a total of 6,526 persons.[3] People with symptoms of schizophrenia in the Danish population, aged 35-45 in 2007, who have never been admitted to a psychiatric hospital, are not included in this data set. Neither are people who will have symptoms of schizophrenia after 2007. However, results show that the vast majority of people with schizophrenia have been admitted with this diagnosis before age 45 (see figure A1). There might also be people who have been admitted with schizophrenia for the first time before 1981 but never since. However, the individuals in this analysis were 9-19 years of age in 1981, and research has shown that only a very few people were admitted with schizophrenia before age 19 (see figure A1).

To construct a sample of siblings, we use the Danish administrative registers on family relations. We select all people with schizophrenia aged 35-45 in 2007 with a sibling of the same sex, with the same mother and father, and with a maximum of 5 years age difference within the age range of 35-45. Another condition is that the sibling has never been in contact with a psychiatric hospital. If several siblings meet this criterion, we choose the sibling who is closest to the person with schizophrenia in age. The definition for siblings implies that the two siblings can largely be assumed to have the same family and social background and other characteristics during childhood. In addition, the two siblings share on average 50 percent identical genes (Plomin, 1986). When selecting siblings of the same gender, we take into account the greater incidence of schizophrenia among men and the likelihood that boys and girls are brought up differently. The people with schizophrenia who have no biological same-sex sibling with a maximum of 5 years age difference are referred to as "people with schizophrenia without siblings" even though they might have a sibling who does not meet our criteria. The sample of siblings consists of 588 pairs, 1,176 individuals, for whom we have complete information on background characteristics and labor market attachment.

The year of admission for the persons with schizophrenia is the year in which they are admitted to a psychiatric hospital or treated as outpatients for the first time

---

3 The selected group of all people aged 35-45 in 2007 is chosen because almost all cases with schizophrenia develop before age 35 and most people in this age group have had the opportunity to complete an education and to find a job. An upper age limit above 45 years would imply more people with schizophrenia in the control group because their first admission could be before year 1981 where the data on admissions to psychiatric hospital were less valid.

with schizophrenia. To be able to compare the siblings in the year of admission, we have defined the year of selection to be the year in which the sibling without schizophrenia was the same age as the sibling with schizophrenia was at admission.

The correlation between schizophrenia and employment might differ across heterogeneous groups. While a first admission at an early age can measure the severity of the illness and loss of human capital leading to a decreased employment, it can also lead to an enhanced employment situation because early identification and treatment may reduce the severity of the disease. The variable age at first admission is defined as a categorical variable with six categories (below 20, 20-25, 25-30, 30-35, above 35, and never admitted). We expect the length of the first admission to express the severity of the illness, leading to a decreased employment rate. The variable length at first admission is defined as a categorical variable with seven categories (less than 1 week, 1 week to 1 month, 1-3 months, 3-6 months, 6-12 months, more than 1 year, and never admitted).

The employment variable is the individuals' labor market status in November 2007 in the Danish register-based labor market statistic (RAS). RAS follows the international guidelines for records on the population's labor market attachment. According to the guidelines for the classification of employment status, work is assigned greater weight than other relations. If a person works only for one hour a week, he or she will still be classified as employed. Almost all individuals in the sample with schizophrenia were discharged from the psychiatric hospital before 2007, the year where the employment status is measured.

We include the following additional control variables in the estimated models. First we control for a list of individual characteristics: age and age squared, that allow for a nonlinear relationship in age, and a dummy variable for male, ethnicity and if the individual is the first born in a family. A person with a sibling having schizophrenia may be affected differently by the ill sibling if he or she is the younger or the older of the two in the sibling pair. Since we use the siblings without schizophrenia as a comparison group, we construct a variable, eldest, indicating who of the two siblings is the eldest. Furthermore, we construct a dummy variable, indicating no biological siblings meeting our criteria (a sibling of same gender, with a maximum of 5 years age difference, that has never been admitted to a psychiatric hospital).

Second, we control for marital status, having at least one child, educational status, work experience, criminal records and region of residence in the year of admission (individuals with schizophrenia) or selection (siblings without schizophrenia). As these variables might be influenced by symptoms related to schizophrenia we show the results with and without these variables.

We define a categorical variable covering all education codes with the outcomes less than 9th grade, 9th grade, high school degree, vocational, short further, medium further, long further education, and unknown education. Moreover, we construct a dummy variable, indicating enrollment into an education as the main occupation, at the time of admission or selection. The continuous variable work experience measure the total number of years the individual had been working before admission or selection.

We define the region of residence into three categories; urban areas, metro areas, and the rest of Denmark. Urban covers Copenhagen and Aarhus, and metropolitan covers the remaining Zealand, Fyn, and central Jutland. Furthermore, we define a dummy variable for at least one criminal record from 1981 to 2007. All types of criminal records with the exception of traffic related records are included, regardless of verdict type.[4]

Finally, we include a variable measuring the number of years from the discharge from the first admission (or selection) to 2007, where the employment status is measured. If an individual is still admitted in 2007 the distance will be zero years.[5]

In Table A1 means and standard deviations are shown for a sample of people with schizophrenia without a sibling, a sample of people with schizophrenia with a sibling, and a sample of people with a sibling with schizophrenia. Standard t-test of differences in means are conducted to determine whether people with schizophrenia with and without siblings have different characteristics, and whether siblings with or without schizophrenia have different characteristics. People with schizophrenia with and without siblings differ significantly on ethnicity, marital status, and living area in the year of admission. Furthermore, among people with schizophrenia without siblings 7% have less than 9th grade and 11% are enrolled into an education. The same percentages among people with schizophrenia with a sibling are 5% and 14%.

Siblings with and without schizophrenia differ significantly on most characteristics (see table A1). Among the siblings with schizophrenia 8% are married, 53% have 9th grade or less as highest educational attainment and 49% have a criminal record. Among siblings without schizophrenia 26% are married, 39% have 9th grade or less as highest educational attainment and 29% have a criminal record.

Table A2 compare the sample of sibling without schizophrenia with the rest of the Danish population in the same age group. The siblings without schizophrenia

---

[4] These include imprisonment, suspended sentence, fine, warning, and containment.
[5] This is only the case for 4 persons with schizophrenia without siblings, and none of the siblings.

differ on average on most characteristics from the rest of the Danish population. For example, among sibling without schizophrenia 66% are men, 96% are ethnic Danes, 53% are married, 64% have children and 25% have 9th grade or less as highest educational attainment. Among the rest of the Danish population 51% are men, 90% are ethnic Danes, 62% are married, 72% have children and 20% have 9th grade or less as highest educational attainment.

To sum up, siblings with and without schizophrenia differ from the whole population with and without schizophrenia on a number of observable characteristics. This difference in observable characteristics is expected, as families with one and more children are likely to differ on several characteristics, and not necessarily a problem, when we estimate the employment rate, if we believe that there are no important non-observable differences between these groups.

To test if the results differ depending on the selected sample we compare our results based on the sibling sample (sample 3) with two samples: a sample including all 6,526 Danes aged 35-45 with schizophrenia and the 588 siblings who have never been admitted to a psychiatric hospital (sample 2) and a sample including all 6,526 Danes aged 35-45 with schizophrenia and the rest of the population in the same age group (sample 1).

Table A3 shows the descriptive statistics for sample 2 and 3. Table A3 also shows differences in means between the two samples corresponding to the differences between people with schizophrenia with and without siblings.

4 Methodological approach

Our empirical goal is to estimate the effect of schizophrenia on employment. The baseline model to estimate individual i's employment rate, *emp*, is expressed as:

(1) $\quad emp_i = \beta w_i + \gamma S_i + u_i$

In equation (1) w is a set of observable characteristics summarizing human and social capital factors. The human and social capital factors are measurements of educational level, size of social network, social competences, parental characteristics, demographics, criminal records, work experience, and health status. Health status covers both physical health and measurements of mental health, not included in schizophrenia. S is the measure of schizophrenia.

As equation (1) controls for indirect effects of schizophrenia that may operate through elements in w, the parameter γ represents the contemporaneous association between schizophrenia and employment. When we estimate the correlation between schizophrenia and the employment rate without controlling for any other factors, γ represent all direct and indirect effects.

Several indirect effects may be important when we estimate the relationship between schizophrenia and the employment rate. Since schizophrenia is related to social withdrawal, schizophrenia can affect, e.g., the probability of being married and having children, factors that often correlate with the probability of being employed. Furthermore, the symptoms related to schizophrenia also include distractibility, concentration difficulties, and reduced memory functioning, and these symptoms might affect the likelihood of completing an education and consequently the likelihood of being employed. Schizophrenia is also often associated with alcoholism and other forms of substance abuse, increasing the likelihood of committing crime, and thereby decreasing the likelihood of being employed. As a consequence of a lower educational attainment and employment in previous periods people with schizophrenia often have less work experience and this factor is a significant factor in explaining the probability of being employed. In section 5.2 we examine potential indirect effects by estimating equation (1) with and without the variable measuring schizophrenia.

We present the results from estimating equation (1) using a linear probability model (LPM). As the employment outcome is binary, we have also estimated all models with a logit model. However, the results are virtually the same. Furthermore, the LPM predicts few of the observations outside the 0-1 interval (see figure A2).

Unobserved factors determining employment are included in the error term, u. If these unobserved factors both influence schizophrenia and the employment, the results, when applying the LPM, could be biased. In this paper we use the sibling pairs to control for unobserved factors shared by siblings, such as family and early environment factors.

When we use siblings the relationship between schizophrenia and employment in 2007 is given by the following model:

(2) $\quad Emp_{i,f} = \beta_0 + \beta_1 \cdot Schizo_{i,f} + \beta_2 \cdot sex_f + \beta_3 \cdot ethnicity_f + \delta \cdot w_{i,f} + u_{i,f}$

(3) $\quad u_{i,f} = \alpha_f + g_f + \varepsilon_{i,f}.$ $\qquad$ i=1,2 and f=1,2,…,588

Index i indicates whether sibling 1 or 2 is considered. Index f indicates the family the sibling belongs to. The interpretation of β_1 is the ceteris paribus effect on the employment rate when an individual goes from having no mental health problems to being diagnosed with schizophrenia. Because β_1 is a binary variable it represents the difference in percentage in the employment rate for people with and without schizophrenia. Gender and ethnicity are restricted to be the same for sibling 1 and 2 making f the only index to these variables.

In equation (3) the error term, $u_{i,f}$, is separated into three components, a family and environmental component, α_f, a genetic component, g_f, and an individual specific error term, ε_{if}. The family and environmental component, α_f, consists of the unobserved factors determining employment and includes factors related to the family environment, parental socioeconomic and neighborhood characteristics. These factors are all shed by the siblings, i.e., they only vary between the families. The individual specific error term, ε_{if}, contains the rest of the sibling's family and social background that varies both between the siblings and the families and all other individual specific factors determining the employment status. These factors include personal characteristics related to schizophrenia such as social withdrawal, distractibility, concentration difficulties, and reduced memory functioning – characteristics that are the diagnostic symptoms of schizophrenia – and these characteristics can also affect the probability of being employed.

The error term consists of a genetic component determining employment, g_f, and is partly the same for the two siblings as they on average share 50 percent of their genes. If there is a genetic component determining employment and it varies both within the sibling-pair and between the families it is included in ε_{if}. Finally, ε_{if} contains all other individual specific components determining employment status that cannot be explained by α_f, g_f, and the covariates.

The vector $w_{i,f}$, in equation (1), contains other possible observed explanatory variables. These are variables measuring age, marital status, first born status, number of children, educational achievements, criminal records, municipality code, work experience before admission or selection, and the distance from being discharged from the first admission to 2007, where the employment is measured.

To test for heterogeneous effects we estimate all models replacing the binary variable for schizophrenia with dummy variables measuring age at and length of the first admission.

5 Results

5.1 The employment rate 15 years before and 10 years after admission or selection

As schizophrenia is a mental illness that usually develops over a long period, individuals with schizophrenia might differ from their siblings with respect to their employment status several years before their first admission to a psychiatric hospital. On average the individuals eventually admitted to a psychiatric hospital with schizophrenia start behaving differently from their siblings, with respect to employment, well before they are admitted to the psychiatric hospital and diagnosed with schizophrenia for the first time. Figure 1 shows that the employment rate differs significantly between the two groups of siblings from up to 15 years before the admission/selection and makes a substantial drop six years before the admission. One year before the first admission there is, again, a drop in the employment rate (approximate 15 percentage point). The difference in the employment rate between siblings with and without schizophrenia from one year after the first admission/ selection until 10 years after is stabilized at approximate 60 percentage point. Siblings with schizophrenia maintain about only 25 percent of the employment rate of the siblings after the first admission. Thus, the symptoms of schizophrenia seem to deteriorate the employment situation gradually and long before the first treatment of the disease. Furthermore, the treatment – the admission – has a stabilizing effect with respect to employment. The stabilized employment rate after admission may relate to the eligibility of disability pension after receiving the diagnosis.

The gradual deterioration of the employment rate before the first admission could be explained by the depreciation in human and social capital which often is an unintended consequence of the symptoms related to schizophrenia. A Finish study

Figure 1 The employment rate for the siblings from 15 years before to 10 years after admission or selection.

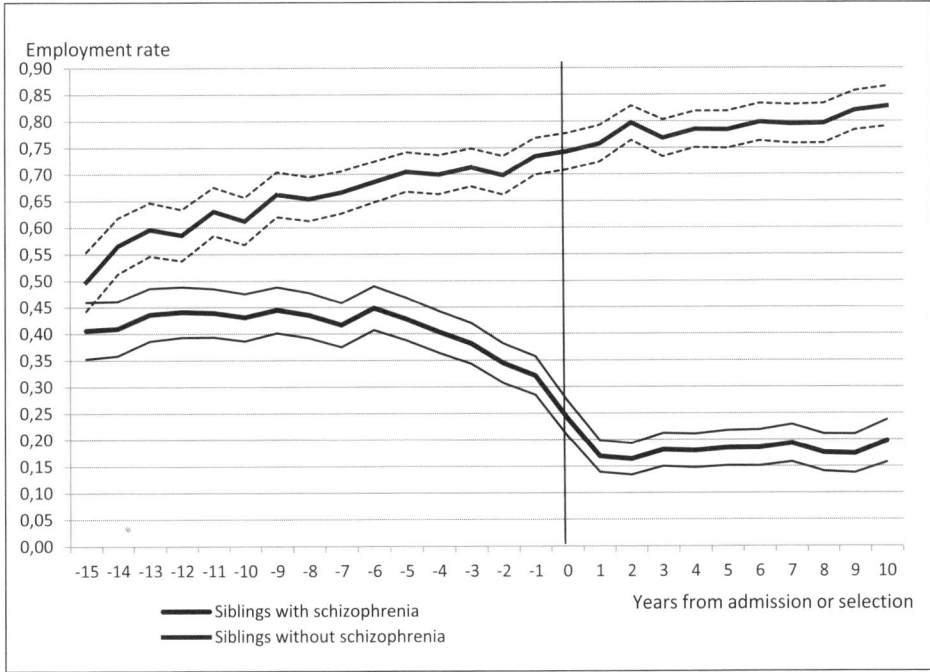

found that although abnormal suspiciousness, sensitivity and difficulties in establishing relationships with peers were characteristics associated with a later development of schizophrenia there were no differences in the academic achievements between children who later developed schizophrenia and a comparable control group (Cannon et al., 1999). Thus, we have no reason to believe, that siblings with and without schizophrenia from birth are differently endowed with abilities to achieve an education. However, differences in nonacademic factors may both have a significant impact on the development of human and social capital and expose individuals with schizophrenia to stigma from the society, leading to a lower employment rate even long before they receive the diagnosis.

5.2 Schizophrenia and employment

Table 1 presents the estimation results for the economic model shown in equation (2). Columns (a), (b), and (c) show the correlation between schizophrenia and employment without controlling for other covariates. Column (a) shows that on average people with schizophrenia are 73.8 percentage points less employed than the rest of the Danish population. The difference in the employment rate between all individuals with schizophrenia and the group of siblings who have never been admitted to a psychiatric hospital is 69.4 percentage points, see column (b). Since the group of people with schizophrenia is the same in (a) and (b), the smaller difference in (b) indicates that siblings to individuals diagnosed with schizophrenia tend to be less employed than the average person in the full sample of all Danes who have never been admitted to a psychiatric hospital. Differences between siblings to people with schizophrenia and the rest of the population are shown in Table A1. Thus, the difference in the results presented in (a) and (b) can partly be explained by observed differences in demographic and socioeconomic characteristics. Moreover, growing up with a sibling with schizophrenia might have a negative influence on educational achievements and later employment outcomes, and this influence might also partly explain the difference in the results presented in (a) and (b).[6]

Column (c) presents the percentage difference in the employment rate for the siblings with and without schizophrenia. The difference is 68.3 percent points and corresponds to the difference in the employment rate between the siblings in Figure 1. When we compare siblings with and without schizophrenia as is done in column (c) we compare siblings with schizophrenia to a group of people who on average have the same socioeconomic background. When we estimate sibling

---

6 Furthermore, medical research of brain scanning show that "healthy" siblings to people with schizophrenia have a higher probability of abnormalities in the brain compared to the rest of the population (Harms et al., 2007).

fixed effects without controlling for other variables we find the same employment effect as in (c).

Column (d) presents the results using sibling fixed effects without controlling for factors which could be influenced by schizophrenia prior to year 2007. The results on the relationship between schizophrenia and employment in column (d) are virtually the same as the results in column (c), namely 67.4 percentage points.

Table 1 Linear probability model results. The relationship schizophrenia and employment.

	(a)	(b)	(c)	(d)	(e)	(f)
Sample	(1)	(2)	(3)	(3)	(3)	(3)
Method	OLS	OLS	OLS	OLS	OLS	Sibling FE
Schizophrenia	-0,738***	-0,694***	-0,673***	-0,675***	-0,555***	-0,547***
	(0,005)	(0,015)	(0,022)	(0,021)	(0,028)	(0,032)
Age in 2007				-0,103	-0,142	-0,299*
				(0,131)	(0,105)	(0,140)
Age^2 in 2007				0,001	0,002	0,003+
				(0,002)	(0,001)	(0,002)
Male					0,046+	
					(0,025)	
Ethnic Dane					0,038	
					(0,073)	
First born				0,063	0,062	0,055
				(0,060)	(0,043)	(0,057)
Eldest of the sibling pair				-0,090	-0,071	-0,073
				(0,077)	(0,043)	(0,073)
Urban areas					0,055*	-0,008
					(0,025)	(0,069)
Metropolitan areas					0,051+	0,035
					(0,029)	(0,056)
Children					-0,001	0,024
					(0,028)	(0,043)
Divorced					-0,050	0,001
					(0,072)	(0,092)
Not married					-0,042	0,014
					(0,034)	(0,052)

Results

	(a)	(b)	(c)	(d)	(e)	(f)
9th grade					0,061	-0,033
					(0,063)	(0,096)
High School					0,068	0,033
					(0,069)	(0,096)
Vocational training					0,041	0,001
					(0,067)	(0,087)
Short further education					0,141+	0,048
					(0,074)	(0,114)
Medium further education					0,150+	0,063
					(0,078)	(0,107)
Long further education					0,181*	0,008
					(0,075)	(0,119)
Unknown education					0,019	-0,169
					(0,082)	(0,127)
Enrolled into an education					0,081*	0,051
					(0,032)	(0,038)
Years from admission or selection					0,015***	0,086
					(0,003)	(0,062)
Years of work experience before admission or selection					0,026***	0,031***
					(0,003)	(0,005)
Criminal records (not traffic)					-0,050*	-0,031
					(0,024)	(0,038)
Constant	0,898***	0,854***	0,854***	2,821	3,367	7,094*
	(0,000)	(0,015)	(0,015)	(2,662)	(2,092)	(3,123)
N	815.158	7.112	1.176	1.176	1.176	1.176
Adj. R-sq	0,04	0,21	0,45	0,63	0,51	0,66

Notes: Sample (1) includes all people with schizophrenia aged 35-45 in 2007 and all people aged 35-45 in 2007 in the Danish population, who never have been in contact with a psychiatric hospital. Sample (2) includes all people with schizophrenia aged 35-45 in 2007 and the sample of relevant siblings to people with schizophrenia. Sample (3) includes people with schizophrenia aged 35-45 in 2007 with a relevant sibling and their siblings.
Significance levels + p<0.1, * p<0.05, ** p<0.01, *** p<0.001.
Robust standard errors in parentheses.

Column (e) and (f) present the results of the correlation between schizophrenia and the employment rate on the sibling sample including other controls. The coefficients on schizophrenia in (c) and (e) illustrates that a number of other covariates partly explain the difference in the employment rate between the sibling pairs. In the LPM using sibling pairs, column (e), the coefficient on schizophrenia is 55.5 percent points.

Several of the additional control variables are significant in explaining the employment. Males have an employment rate 4.6 percentage points higher than females (only significant at a 10 percent level). Individuals living in urban or metropolitan areas in the year of selection or admission have an employment rate approximately 5 percentage points higher than the individuals living in the rest of Denmark. People with short, medium, and long further education have, a 14, 15, and 18 percentage points higher employment rate, respectively, than people with less than 9th grade. The variables indicating short and medium further education are significant at a 10 percent level. People enrolled into an education, in the year of admission or selection, have 8 percentage points higher employment rate in 2007 than the individuals with less than 9th grade. People with criminal records have, 5 percentage points lower employment rate than people with no records.

Number of years since first admission/selection is associated with an increase in the employment rate. This result could be driven by the siblings without schizophrenia who face an increasing employment rate over time as illustrated in Figure 1. Each year of work experience increases the employment rate by 2.6 percentage points.

Column (f) presents the results on the effect of schizophrenia on employment using the sibling fixed effects (FE) approach. This approach estimates a significant difference in the employment rate at 54.7 percentage points. This difference in the employment rate is virtually the same as the one we found using the LPM approach in column (e), indicating that unobserved factors shared by the siblings are not important when we estimate the relationship between schizophrenia and employment.

Results in Table 1 show that the estimated effect of schizophrenia on employment is much larger when we do not control for indirect effects such as education, work experience etc. In Table A4 we exclude the binary variable measuring schizophrenia in the first three columns and show the relationship between all other included covariates and employment. In the last three columns we include the variable measuring schizophrenia. The changes in the parameter estimates on all the other controls indicate the variables through which schizophrenia affects employment. The parameter estimates that change when we include the binary indicator for schizophrenia are measuring: to have children, to be married, to have a further education, to have more years with work experience, and to have a criminal record. These results suggest that the relationship between schizophrenia and employment we find in Table 1, columns (a) – (d), partly are explained by these factors.

5.3 Age at First Admission

In Table 2 the binary variable for schizophrenia shown in Table 1 is replaced with categories for age at first admission and people who have never been admitted as reference group. The additional control variables presented in Table 1, column (e) and (f) are also included in the models shown in Table 2, column (e) and (f), but are left out of the table for brevity.

Table 2, column (a) presents the difference in the probability of being employed between all individuals with schizophrenia and the rest of the population. Table 2, column (b) presents the difference in employment in the probability of being employed between all individuals with schizophrenia and the group of siblings (without schizophrenia). In both columns (a) and (b) we see that the difference in the employment rate increase with an older age at the first treatment. However, the parameter estimates for the different age groups are in most cases not statistically significant from each other. This later result applies in column (a) and (b) and in the other columns in Table 2.

The results in column (b) show that those who are being treated for the first time when they are less than 20 years, have an employment rate which is 65.8 percentage points lower than the siblings without schizophrenia. Among those who are being treated for the first time when they are over 35 years, however, the employment rate is 70.6 percentage points lower than the siblings without schizophrenia.

When we control for a number of characteristics that may affect the probability of being employed, such as age, marital status, education and work experience, the difference in the employment probability between individuals with schizophrenia and their siblings without schizophrenia is 53 percentage points for those who are being treated with schizophrenia for the first time when they are less than 20 years, between 20 and 25, and over 35 years, see column (e).[7] The difference in employment probability is significantly higher (64 percentage points) if the sibling with schizophrenia were admitted between ages 25-30.[8] The difference in employment probability of the siblings who were hospitalized for the first time

---

7 F-tests of coefficients: H_0: Age below 20=Age 20-25= Age above 35, P=0.997. H_0: Age below 20=Age 20-25=Age 30-35=Age above 35, P=0.957.
8 F-tests of coefficients: H_0: Age below 20 – Age 25-30=0, P=0.077. H_0: Age 20-25 – Age 25-30=0, P=0.011. H_0: Age 30-35 – Age 25-30=0, P=0.002. H_0: Age above 35 – Age 25-30=0, P=0.038.

when they were between 30 and 35 years is 51 percentage points, and this difference only differ significantly from the age group 25-30 years. When we include other controls that may affect employment, the difference in the results using OLS and sibling fixed effects methods is smaller than when these controls are omitted.

Table 2 Linear probability model results. The relationship between age first admission to psychiatric hospital, diagnosed with schizophrenia, and employment.

	(a)	(b)	(c)	(d)	(e)	(f)
Sample	(1)	(2)	(3)	(3)	(3)	(3)
Method	OLS	OLS	OLS	Sibling FE	OLS	Sibling FE
Addition control variables	No	No	No	No	Yes	Yes
Age under 20	-0,702***	-0,658***	-0,607***	-0,562***	-0,534***	-0,510***
	(0,016)	(0,021)	(0,053)	(0,067)	(0,057)	(0,069)
Age 20-25	-0,732***	-0,688***	-0,632***	-0,639***	-0,533***	-0,567***
	(0,010)	(0,018)	(0,038)	(0,045)	(0,041)	(0,046)
Age 25-30	-0,739***	-0,695***	-0,760***	-0,763***	-0,641***	-0,624***
	(0,009)	(0,017)	(0,027)	(0,034)	(0,033)	(0,042)
Age 30-35	-0,746***	-0,702***	-0,642***	-0,623***	-0,508***	-0,445***
	(0,009)	(0,017)	(0,036)	(0,045)	(0,043)	(0,05)
Age over 35	-0,750***	-0,706***	-0,704***	-0,783***	-0,528***	-0,533***
	(0,011)	(0,018)	(0,048)	(0,058)	(0,059)	(0,075)
Constant	0,898***	0,854***	0,854***	0,854	3,660+	7,022*
	(0,000)	(0,015)	(0,011)	(0,784)	(2,090)	(3,050)
N	815.158	7.112	1.176	1.176	1.176	1.176
Adj. R-sq	0,04	0,21	0,46	0,64	0,51	0,67

Notes: Sample (1) includes all people with schizophrenia aged 35-45 in 2007 and all people aged 35-45 in 2007 in the Danish population who never have been in contact with a psychiatric hospital. Sample (2) includes all people with schizophrenia aged 35-45 in 2007 and the sample of relevant siblings to people with schizophrenia. Sample (3) includes people with schizophrenia aged 35-45 in 2007 with a relevant sibling and their siblings.
The additional control variables shown in Table 1 are included in colum (e) and (f) but not shown.
Significance levels + $p<0.1$, * $p<0.05$, ** $p<0.01$, *** $p<0.001$.
Robust standard errors in parentheses.

In summary, the results indicate that the difference in the employment rates between siblings with and without schizophrenia is higher than average, if siblings with schizophrenia are hospitalized for the first time when they are between 25 and 30 years. Besides this age-category, the differences in the employment rate for the different age groups are similar to the finding in the previous section. Therefore, the results showing the difference in the employment rate between siblings with and without schizophrenia seem to be relatively robust to different ages at the first admission to a psychiatric hospital.

5.4 Length of First Admission

In Table 3 the binary variable for schizophrenia is replaced with categories for the length of the first admission with people never been admitted as reference group. Table 3, column (a) and (b) show only minor difference in employment rate for different length of first admission. However, there seems to be a tendency that a longer duration of the first admission is associated with higher differences in the employment rate. In Table 3, column (c) and (d) the results are estimated with OLS and sibling fixed effects method, respectively, on the sample containing siblings only. These results present an inverted U-shaped relationship between length of first hospitalization and employment. The group who are hospitalized more than one year, have a smaller difference in the employment probability (65.6 percentage points) than those who were hospitalized 6 to 12 months (70.4 percentage points).

For those who were hospitalized less than a week the difference between parameters estimated with OLS (57.9) and siblings fixed effects (64.1) indicate that family factors that are shared between siblings affect estimation of the employment probability when we use the OLS approach.

In column (e) and (f) we control for a number of additional controls affecting the probability of being employed. The results in these columns show that the difference in the employment rate varies over the length of the first hospitalization and have an inverted u-shaped relationship. The largest difference in employment rates are when siblings diagnosed with schizophrenia were hospitalized between three and six months. Among individuals who have been hospitalized three to six months, the employment rate is 60.8 percentage points less than their siblings who have never been hospitalized, see column (e). This difference in employment rate is considerably higher than it is for people who have been hospitalized one week to one month and more than one year (48.1 and 49.9 percentage points, respectively).[9]

---

9 F-test: H_0: "<=1 week" ="3-6 months", P=0.024 and H_0: "3-6 months" = ">1 year", P=0.016.

Besides the length of admission of three to six months, all coefficients for the different lengths of admissions are virtually the same[10] and the coefficients are all close to the average difference in the employment rate at 55.5 percent points, see Table 1, column (e).

Table 3 Linear probability model results. The relationship between length of stay at first admission to a psychiatric hospital, diagnosed with schizophrenia, and employment.

	(a)	(b)	(c)	(d)	(e)	(f)
Sample	(1)	(2)	(3)	(3)	(3)	(3)
Method	OLS	OLS	OLS	Sibling FE	OLS	Sibling FE
Addition control variables	No	No	No	No	Yes	Yes
<=1 week	-0,730***	-0,467***	-0,579***	-0,641***	-0,481***	-0,493***
	(0,016)	(0,023)	(0,072)	(0,077)	(0,063)	(0,080)
1 week-1 month	-0,720***	-0,458***	-0,617***	-0,618***	-0,473***	-0,464***
	(0,016)	(0,023)	(0,058)	(0,079)	(0,058)	(0,078)
1-3 months	-0,735***	-0,472***	-0,638***	-0,632***	-0,531***	-0,520***
	(0,010)	(0,019)	(0,040)	(0,049)	(0,043)	(0,052)
3-6 months	-0,735***	-0,472***	-0,704***	-0,721***	-0,608***	-0,602***
	(0,011)	(0,020)	(0,034)	(0,044)	(0,036)	(0,048)
6-12 months	-0,742***	-0,480***	-0,686***	-0,702***	-0,548***	-0,538***
	(0,011)	(0,020)	(0,040)	(0,047)	(0,043)	(0,052)
>1 year	-0,750***	-0,487***	-0,646***	-0,686***	-0,499***	-0,496***
	(0,008)	(0,018)	(0,036)	(0,045)	(0,040)	(0,054)
Constant	0,897***	0,635***	0,835***	0,844***	3,253	4,769
	(0,000)	(0,016)	(0,015)	(0,010)	(2,078)	(3,162)
N	815.158	7.112	1.176	1.176	1.176	1.176
Adj. R-sq	0,04	0,14	0,43	0,62	0,50	0,66

Notes: Sample (1) includes all people with schizophrenia aged 35-45 in 2007 and all people aged 35-45 in 2007 in the Danish population who never have been in contact with a psychiatric hospital. Sample (2) includes all people with schizophrenia aged 35-45 in 2007 and the sample of relevant siblings to people with schizophrenia. Sample (3) includes people with schizophrenia aged 35-45 in 2007 with a relevant sibling and their siblings.
The additional control variables shown in Table 1 are included but not shown.
Significance levels + $p<0.1$, * $p<0.05$, ** $p<0.01$, *** $p<0.001$.
Robust standard errors in parentheses.

---

10 F-tests: P-values between 0.103-0.919.

6. Discussion

Schizophrenia is a severe and complex mental disorder that often has serious disabling consequences for the affected individual. This paper showed that schizophrenic patients are less employed up to 15 years before the first admission to a psychiatric hospital than their siblings, who have never been admitted to a psychiatric hospital. The difference in the employment rate between the siblings before admission is likely to be related to the symptoms related to schizophrenia which often lead to a depreciation of both human and social capital. Also, difficulties in establishing social relationships, a symptom related to schizophrenia, can expose the individuals diagnosed with schizophrenia to stigma from the society and employees. It remains a possible explanation that a job loss may trigger schizophrenia because a job loss can be associated with the loss of the work values, lack of self-confidence, stress and resignation. However, this reverse causality seems to be less important.

As schizophrenia usually has an early onset age and the development is likely to be affected by fragile family relations, unobserved family specific characteristics is likely to be part of the explanation for the negative relationship between schizophrenia and employment. In this paper we used a sibling fixed effects approach to eliminate bias in the relationship between schizophrenia and employment due to unobserved family characteristics. The results show that unobservable family characteristics are not important when we estimate the relationship between schizophrenia and employment. However, when we examine the relationship between age at and length of first admission the shared family factors may influence the relationship between these indicators and the probability of being employed.

We were not able to control for other unobserved individual specific characteristics that might affect both the probability of developing schizophrenia and the probability of being employed. However, results from a Finnish study showed that children who later were diagnosed with schizophrenia, on average, did not achieve different results in school compared to a similar group of children who never developed schizophrenia (Cannon et al., 1999). This results indicates that siblings with and without schizophrenia, on average, do not differ in the innate abilities of learning. Thus, the unobservable individual characteristics are more likely to be related to the symptoms related to schizophrenia.

7. Conclusion

In this paper we use Danish administrative register data to examine the relationship between schizophrenia and employment. With these data we were able to compare people with schizophrenia with their siblings who were never hospitalized. The results show that the employment rate differ significantly between siblings with and without schizophrenia from up to 15 years before the first admission to a psychiatric hospital. For the siblings diagnosed with schizophrenia the drop in the employment rate was substantial 6 years before the first hospital admission. After the first hospital admission, the employment rate stabilizes and approximately 18 percent of the siblings with schizophrenia are employed in the following 10 years.

When we estimate the relationship between schizophrenia and employment in 2007 the results showed a difference in the employment rate on 67 percentage points. This result is the direct effect of schizophrenia. When we include additional control variables such as marital status, educational achievement and work experience the difference in the employment rate is reduced to 56 percentage points. This result remains almost unchanged in the sibling fixed effects approach, indicating that the coefficient to schizophrenia is not biased due to unobserved family heterogeneity.

The robustness of the average correlation between schizophrenia and employment was investigated by two more flexible specifications for schizophrenia, age at and length of the first admission to a psychiatric hospital. We found that the average difference in the employment rate was relatively robust in these more flexible specifications. However, the difference in the employment rate was larger than average when the individuals were admitted between age 25 and 30, i.e., 64.1 percentage points.

The results in this paper suggest that schizophrenia is linked to a large reduction in labor market participation. Most of the reduction in employment rate happens well before this group has the first admission to a psychiatric hospital and before they are diagnosed with schizophrenia. This result could be relevant for preventive policies in the future. The decrease in the employment rate before the group is diagnosed with schizophrenia indicates a productivity loss from the illness through depreciation of human and social capital. The more the human and social capital depreciate, the more the individual becomes alienated from the labor market or simply loses his or her contacts within it. Thus, beyond the immediate reduction in direct costs, effective treatments used early in the course of schizophrenia could have important effects on later labor market participation.

References

Agerbo E, Byrne M, Eaton W, Mortensen P B. Marital and labor market status in the long run in schizophrenia. Archives of General Psychiatry, 2004; 61(1); 28(6).

Andlin-Sobocki P, Jönsson B, Wittchen H.-U, Olesen J. Cost of disorders of the brain in Europe, European Journal of Neurology, 2005; 12 (Suppl. 1); 1–27.

Bartel A, Taubman P. Health and Labor Market Success: The Role of Various Diseases. The Review of Economics and Statistics, 1979; 61; 1-8.

Bates P. Stuff as dreams are made of. Health Service Journal 33:5497.

Cannon M, Jones P, Huttunen M O, Tanskanen A, Huttunen T, Rabe-Hesketh S, Murray R M. School Performance in Finnish Children and Later Development of Schizophrenia. Archives of general psychiatry, 1999; 56(5); 457-463.

Chatterji P A, Alegria M, Takeuchi D. Psychiatric disorders and labor market outcomes: Evidence from the National Comorbidity Survey-Replication. Journal of Health Economics, 2011; 30(5); 858-868.

Christensen T, Nordentoft M. "Review om effekter af beskæftigelsesindsatser til personer med svær psykisk sygdom". http://bmhandicap.dk/Inspirationpct.20ogpct.20Fakta/Rapporter.aspx

Ettner SL, Frank RG, Kessler RC. The impact of psychiatric disorders on labor market outcomes. Industrial and Labor Relations Review, 1997; 51(1); 64-81.

Greve J. "Et liv i periferien: Levevilkår, behandling og samfundsdeltagelse blandt danskere med svære sindslidelser." Rockwool Foundation Research Unit. 2012.

Hatfield B, Huxley P, Mohamad H. Accommodation and employment: A survey into the circumstances and expressed needs of users of mental health services in a Northern Town. British Journal of Social Work. 1992. 22(1):61–73.

Harms M P, Wang L, Mamah D, Barch D M, Thompson P A, Csernansky J G. Thalamic shape abnormalities in individuals with schizophrenia and their nonpsychotic siblings. The Journal of Neuroscience, 2007; 27(50); 13835-13842.

Heckman J, Masterov D V. The productivity argument for investing in young children, Review of Agricultural Economics, 2007; 29(3): 446-493.

Jacobsen C B, Martin H M, Andersen S L, Christensen R N, Bengtsson S. "Stigma og psykiske lidelser som det opleves og opfattes af mennesker med psykiske lidelser og borgere i Danmark". Report. Danske Regioner, DSI and SFI, 2010.

Laursen T M, Nordentoft M, Gissler M, Westman J, Vahlbeck K. "Psykiatrisk forskning i Norden. En beskrivelse af forskningsmuligheder i psykiatri-relevante register i Danmark, Sverige og Finland". *NHV-rapport 2010:11.*

McLaughlin K, Breslau J, Green J G, Lakoma M D, Sampson N A, Zaslavsky A M, Kessler R C. Childhood socio-economic status and the onset, persistence, and severity of DSM-IV mental disorders in a US national sample. Social Science & Medicine, 2011, 73(7), 1088-1096.

Marcotte D E, Wilcox-Gök V. Estimating the employment and earnings costs of mental illness: recent developments in the United States. Social Science & Medicine, 2001; 53(1); 21-27.

Marwaha S, Johnson S. Schizophrenia and Employment. A Review. Soc. Psychiatry Psychiatr. Epidemiol. 2004. 39: 337-349.

Mors O, Perto G P, Mortensen P B. The Danish Psychiatric Central Research Register. Scandinavian Journal of Public Health, 2011; 39 (Suppl. 7); 54–57.

Nordentoft M. "Skizofreni og Psykose – Symptomer, forløb og prognose". In: Nordentoft M, Melau M, Iversen T, Kjær S. Psykose for unge. Symptomer behandling og fremtid. Psykiatrifondens forlag. 2009.

Plomin, R. Development, Genetics, and Psychology. Lawrence Erlbaum Associates, Inc., Publishers. 1986.

Sham P C, MacLean C J, Kendler K S. A typological model of schizophrenia based on age at onset, sex and familial morbidity. Acta Psychiatr Scand, 1994; 89(2); 135-141.

Westergaard-Nielsen N, Agerbo E, Eriksson T, Mortensen P B. Mental illness: Gender differences with respect to marital status and labour market outcomes. In: Marcotte, D. E. (ed.) The Economics of Gender and Mental Illness; Research in Human Capital and Development, vol. 15, Emerald Group Publishing Limited; 2004. p. 73-94.

Appendix

Figure A1 Cumulated frequencies of first admissions with schizophrenia over age by gender, year 1994-2010

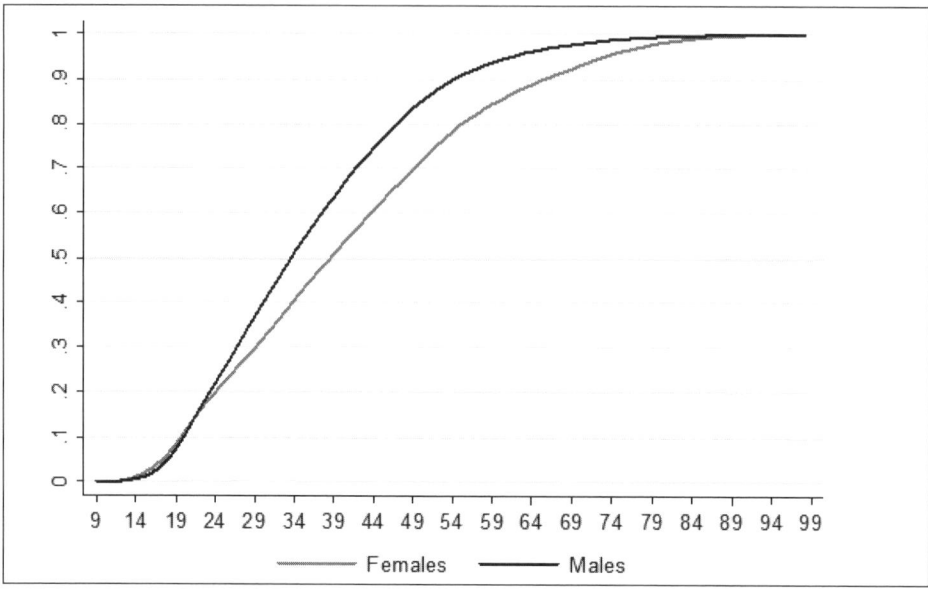

Figure A2 Predicted cumulated density function for employment rate for the linear probabiliy model in Table 1 column (e) and a logistic regression including the same variables, on sample 3.

Table A1 Descriptive Statistics, mean and standard deviations (Std. Dev).

	No siblings, schizophrenic		Siblings, schizophrenic		Siblings, never admitted	
	Mean	Std. Dev.	Mean	Std. Dev.	Mean	Std. Dev.
Measured in year 2007						
Age	40.25	3.08	40.13	2.80	40.47*	2.73
Male	0.64	0.48	0.66	0.47	0.66	0.47
Ethnic Dane	0.86***	0.35	0.96	0.19	0.96	0.19
First born	0.78***	0.41	0.38	0.47	0.48**	0.50
Eldest in the sibling pair	0.00***	0.00	0.45	0.50	0.55**	0.50
No sibling pair	1.00***	0.00	0.00	0.00	0.00	0.00
Measured in the year of admission or selection						
Living in urban areas	0.54***	0.50	0.46	0.50	0.47	0.50
Living in metropolitan areas	0.24*	0.43	0.28	0.45	0.26	0.44
Living in the rest of DK	0.22*	0.41	0.26	0.44	0.27	0.45
Children	0.17	0.38	0.19	0.39	0.45***	0.50
Married	0.13***	0.34	0.08	0.27	0.26***	0.44
Divorced	0.07*	0.26	0.04	0.21	0.02**	0.13
Not married	0.80***	0.40	0.88	0.33	0.72***	0.45
Less than 9th grade	0.07*	0.26	0.05	0.22	0.03	0.18
9th grade	0.44+	0.50	0.48	0.50	0.33***	0.47
High School	0.15	0.36	0.16	0.37	0.16	0.37
Vocational training	0.19	0.39	0.20	0.40	0.29***	0.45
Short further education	0.02	0.15	0.01	0.12	0.05**	0.21
Medium further education	0.04	0.21	0.04	0.19	0.08**	0.27
Long further education	0.02	0.13	0.02	0.13	0.04*	0.20
Unknown education	0.06+	0.23	0.04	0.19	0.01**	0.12
Enrolled into an education	0.11*	0.31	0.14	0.35	0.20*	0.40
Measured over various time periods						
Crime (not traffic) 1981-2007	0.51	0.50	0.49	0.50	0.29***	0.46
Years from admission or selection	10.34***	6.61	11.71	6.53	12.02	6.55
Years of work experience before admission or selection	5.16*	4.88	5.61	4.65	9.01***	5.74
N	5,936		588		588	

Notes: Standard t-test of differences in means is conducted between people with schizophrenia with and without siblings and between siblings with and without schizophrenia. Significance levels + p<0.1, * p<0.05, ** p<0.01, *** p<0.001.
The samples include all people aged 35-45 in 2007.

Table A2 Descriptive statistics for people aged 35-45 in 2007, who have never been admitted to a psychiatric hospital. Mean and standard deviation (Std. dev.)

	Siblings, never admitted		Rest of the population, never admitted	
	Mean	Std. dev.	Mean	Std. dev.
Age in years	40.4**	2.74	40.04	3.10
Male	0.66***	0.47	0.51	0.50
Ethnic Dane	0.96***	0.19	0.90	0.30
Urban areas	0.44*	0.50	0.39	0.49
Metropolitan areas	0.32*	0.47	0.36	0.48
Children	0.64***	0.48	0.72	0.45
Married	0.53***	0.50	0.62	0.49
Divorced	0.09	0.29	0.10	0.30
Not married	0.37***	0.48	0.27	0.44
9th grade or less education	0.25**	0.43	0.20	0.40
High School	0.05	0.22	0.07	0.25
Vocational training	0.34***	0.47	0.41	0.49
Short further education	0.08	0.27	0.07	0.25
Medium further education	0.16	0.37	0.17	0.38
Long further education	0.12**	0.33	0.09	0.29
N	588		813,712	

Notes: Standard t-test of differences in means is conducted between siblings never admitted and the rest of the population, never admitted to a psychiatric hospital. Significance levels + $p<0.1$, * $p<0.05$, ** $p<0.01$, *** $p<0.001$.

Table A3 Summary statistics, sample 2 and 3 mean and standard deviation (Std.dev.)

	Sample 2		Sample 3	
Variable	Mean	Std. dev.	Mean	Std. dev.
Age in 2007	40.26	3.03	40.30	2.77
Male	0.64	0.48	0.66	0.47
Danish	0.87*	0.33	0.96	0.19
First born	0.72*	0.45	0.43	0.50
Urban areas	0.53*	0.50	0.46	0.50
Metropolitan areas	0.25	0.43	0.27	0.44
Rest of Denmark	0.22*	0.42	0.27	0.44
Children	0.19*	0.40	0.32	0.46
Married	0.14*	0.34	0.17	0.38
Divorced	0.06*	0.24	0.03	0.17
Not married	0.80	0.40	0.80	0.40
Less than 9th grade	0.07*	0.25	0.04	0.20
9th grade	0.44*	0.50	0.41	0.49
High School	0.15	0.36	0.16	0.37
Vocational	0.20*	0.40	0.24	0.43
Short further education	0.02	0.15	0.03	0.17
Medium further education	0.05	0.21	0.06	0.23
Long further education	0.02	0.14	0.03	0.17
Unknown education	0.05*	0.22	0.03	0.16
Enrolled into an education	0.12*	0.33	0.17	0.38
Crime (not traffic)	10.59*	6.62	11.86	6.54
Years from admission	5.51*	5.05	7.31	5.49
N	7,112		1,176	

Notes: Sample 2 includes all people with schizophrenia aged 35-45 in 2007 and the sample of relevant siblings to people with schizophrenia. Sample 3 includes people with schizophrenia aged 35-45 in 2007 with a relevant sibling and their siblings.
Standard t-test of differences in means is conducted between sample 2 and 3. Significance levels * p<0.05.

Table A4 The probability of being employed. With and without controlling for schizophrenia. Linear probability model. Robust standard errors in parentheses.

Sample	2	3	3	2	3	3
Method	OLS	OLS	Sibling FE	OLS	OLS	Sibling FE
Schizophrenia				-0.577***	-0.555***	-0.547***
				(0.022)	(0.028)	(0.032)
Age in 2007	-0.0289	-0.159	-0.366*	-0.0242	-0.142	-0.299*
	(0.040)	(0.121)	(0.183)	(0.039)	(0.105)	(0.140)
Age^2 in 2007	0.000226	0.00175	0.00381+	0.000181	0.00163	0.00276+
	(0.001)	(0.002)	(0.002)	(0.000)	(0.001)	(0.002)
Male	0.0291**	0.0576*		0.0221*	0.0462+	
	(0.010)	(0.029)		(0.010)	(0.025)	
Ethnic Dane	-0.0276+	0.0267		-0.0237	0.0381	
	(0.015)	(0.084)		(0.015)	(0.073)	
First born	0.0178	0.0679	0.0771	0.0147	0.062	0.0553
	(0.011)	(0.052)	(0.078)	(0.011)	(0.043)	(0.057)
Eldest of the sibling pair	0.0254	-0.0449	-0.101	-0.0214	-0.0706	-0.0725
	(0.028)	(0.054)	(0.093)	(0.023)	(0.043)	(0.073)
No siblings	-0.265***			-0.0173		
	(0.021)			(0.021)		
Urban areas	0.0187+	0.0774*	-0.00459	0.0157	0.0548*	-0.00819
	(0.011)	(0.031)	(0.077)	(0.011)	(0.025)	(0.069)
Metropolitan areas	0.0103	0.0428	-0.00680	0.0124	0.0513+	0.0351
	(0.013)	(0.034)	(0.069)	(0.012)	(0.029)	(0.056)
Children	0.0329*	0.105**	0.204***	0.00359	-0.00129	0.0237
	(0.013)	(0.032)	(0.049)	(0.012)	(0.028)	(0.043)
Divorced	-0.0425*	-0.221**	-0.140	-0.0178	-0.0497	0.00078
	(0.020)	(0.075)	(0.096)	(0.019)	(0.072)	(0.092)
Not married	-0.0395*	-0.101*	-0.0173	-0.0168	-0.0422	0.0138
	(0.016)	(0.040)	(0.066)	(0.015)	(0.034)	(0.052)
9th grade	0.0365*	0.0810	-0.0371	0.0379**	0.0611	-0.0327
	(0.015)	(0.067)	(0.098)	(0.014)	(0.063)	(0.087)
High School	0.0632***	0.108	0.122	0.0597***	0.0681	0.0326
	(0.018)	(0.073)	(0.113)	(0.019)	(0.069)	(0.096)

Vocational training	0.0298+	0.0748	0.0841	0.0269	0.0413	0.000786
	(0.017)	(0.071)	(0.100)	(0.017)	(0.067)	(0.087)
Short further education	0.158***	0.299***	0.340*	0.130***	0.141+	0.0482
	(0.034)	(0.090)	(0.132)	(0.033)	(0.074)	(0.114)
Medium further education	0.142***	0.220**	0.213+	0.127***	0.150+	0.0631
	(0.027)	(0.085)	(0.123)	(0.026)	(0.078)	(0.107)
Long further education	0.179***	0.295***	0.213	0.153***	0.181*	0.00835
	(0.036)	(0.083)	(0.132)	(0.035)	(0.075)	(0.119)
Unknown education	0.0646**	-0.00276	-0.320*	0.0641**	0.019	-0.169
	(0.021)	(0.097)	(0.147)	(0.021)	(0.082)	(0.127)
Enrolled into an education	0.0851***	0.135***	0.150*	0.0763***	0.0814*	0.0506
	(0.016)	(0.038)	(0.060)	(0.015)	(0.032)	(0.040)
Years from admission or selection	0.0104***	0.0273***	0.0833	0.0085***	0.0146***	0.0858
	(0.010)	(0.003)	(0.071)	(0.001)	(0.003)	(0.062)
Years of work experience before admission or selection	0.0244***	0.0468***	0.0686***	0.0206***	0.0261***	0.0305***
	(0.001)	(0.003)	(0.005)	(0.001)	(0.003)	(0.005)
Criminal records (not traffic)	-0.070***	-0.105***	-0.166***	-0.060***	-0.0499*	-0.0306
	(0.010)	(0.029)	(0.048)	(0.009)	(0.024)	(0.038)
Constant	0.969	3.272	7.520+	1.211	3.367	7.094*
	(0.809)	(2.417)	(3.970)	(0.778)	(2.092)	(3.123)
N	7,112	1,176	1,176	7,112	1,176	1,176
Adj. R-sq	0.20	0.28	0.44	0.28	0.51	0.66

Notes: Sample (2) includes all people with schizophrenia aged 35-45 in 2007 and the sample of relevant siblings to people with schizophrenia. Sample (3) includes people with schizophrenia aged 35-45 in 2007 with a relevant sibling and their siblings.
Significance levels: + $p<0.1$, * $p<0.05$, ** $p<0.01$, *** $p<0.001$.